THE PUT-DOWNS AND INSULTS BIBLE

Witty One-liners & Bitchy Barbs for Every Occasion

THE PUT-DOWNS AND INSULTS BIBLE

Witty One-liners & Bitchy Barbs for Every Occasion

By Ruth Graham   Cartoons by Gill Toft

www.knowthescorebooks.com

Know The Score Books Limited
118 Alcester Road
Studley
Warwickshire
B80 7NT
01527 454482
info@knowthescorebooks.com

A CIP catalogue record is available for this book from the British Library   ISBN: 978-1-905449-20-0

Jacket and book design by Lisa David
Cartoons by Gill Toft

Printed and bound in Great Britain by Martins The Printer

"A graceful taunt is worth a
thousand insults."

– Louis Nizer

"But a good insult stays for life,
not just for Christmas."

~ Ruth Graham

CONTENTS

International Insults

BORN TO BE MILD,
OR SPAWNED TO SPIT FIRE?

Take the quiz on the following pages and find out what you probably already know, but your friends daren't tell you!

Molly clearly didn't understand what her friend meant by 'wear something more your own age'.

Question 1

You go round to collect your middle-aged female friend for a night out. She's dressed in a mini skirt and stretchy low-cut top, and asks how she looks. It's apparent she resembles a lycra zeppelin, but what do you reply?

a) 'Well I'm not saying you look fat, but what label's that skirt? Is it House of Lard?'
b) 'You look great when you stand to the side'.
c) 'To be honest, you'd look lovely in something a bit more 'our' age. Have we still got time to change?'
d) Tell her she looks great. You don't want to hurt her feelings, but you also secretly feel a bit guilty at the thought of all the attention you'll be enjoying.

Question 2

You hear a salacious rumour about an acquaintance. Do you

a) Repeat it, to everyone you know.
b) Wait to find out a bit more before forming a decision.
c) Embellish it, and finish off with 'and the worst thing is, the goat was on tablets for a week afterwards too'.
d) Tell the acquaintance there's something unpleasant being said about them, and then help them to get to the bottom of it.

Question 3

You're at a party when a new couple break into your social circle and start chatting. What happens next?

a) You think 'how lovely' – new people to liven things up.
b) You've sized up her hips, cleavage and legs in a nanosecond and then spend the next 15 minutes distracting your man's eyes to another direction.
c) You say 'sorry – hope you don't mind. We're just in the middle of a really personal chat', even though you were only talking about the X-Factor
d) You all turn your backs – there's no room for invaders.

Question 4

A girl you don't know pops in to a friend's house while you're both having coffee. You're not keen, but make the best of it. After she's gone, what happens?

a) There's silence, but you're determined not to break it and say something horrible.
b) You blurt out 'God – she's hard work'
c) You're subtle, saying something like 'What an interesting selection of friends you have Lucy'.
d) You can't resist it. You just have to sigh dramatically and say 'Well. Today was a waste of make-up'.

Question 5

An ex-partner starts dating someone new. Do you

a) Stick pictures of him in a perished rubber jockstrap
   and nipple clamps on You Tube.
b) Breathe a sigh of relief. Now you really will have to
   face moving on – best thing all round really.
c) Text him and say you've heard she's had more
   hands up her than a glove puppet, and what is he
   thinking?
d) Wish him all the best, although it's killing you.

Question 6

At work, you're asked to make recommendations for someone to 'support' your position. Do you

a) Find the best candidate for the job. Full stop.
b) Find someone adequate, but not too good – you don't want them usurping you eventually.
c) Refuse to help, saying you have enough to do, and besides, you don't need support.
d) Launch an initiative or new campaign to promote new talent and encourage everyone – it's for the good of the company.

Question 7

A friend forgets your birthday. Do you

a) Hold it against them. Forever.
b) Write it off – we're all busy and we all forget things every now and again.
c) Just get a card on their birthday, but make sure it's a cheap embossed one from the market, and don't ever buy them a present again.
d) Ring them up and say it's not like them to forget – and are they okay?

Answers:

Question 1
a = 1 point; b = 2 points; c = 4 points; d = 3 points

Question 2
a = 2 points; b = 4 points; c = 1 point; d = 3 points

Question 3
a = 4 points; b = 3 points; c = 2 points; d = 1 point

Question 4
a = 4 points; b = 2 points; c = 3 points; d = 1 point

Question 5
a = 1 point; b = 4 points; c = 2 points; d = 3 points

Question 6
a = 2 points; b = 3 points; c = 4 points; d = 1 point

Question 7
a = 4 points; b = 2 points; c = 3 points; d = 1 point

Mostly 4's

You're an out-and-out bitch. You probably don't need this book, but will love finding new material in here to try and score one over on people with.

Mostly 3's

You're a bitch by stealth – never directly insulting people, but relaying information that you've 'heard' that people have supposedly done. Backhanded insults will be your forté – read on and stock up!

Mostly 2's

You're like most normal people. You try to be a nice person most of the time, but can't help the halo slipping occasionally. It's human, so there's no harm in selecting a few insults for use on people who truly deserve it – it won't kill you.

Mostly 1's

You're a really nice person who wouldn't dream of being horrible about anyone or anything – ever. Life just isn't like that, so you may find yourself constantly disappointed by other people's attitudes. Don't be afraid to put your toe in the water occasionally, but start with witty rather than bitchy, otherwise the shock impact will work against you.

THE CHARGE OF THE SPITE BRIGADE

Classic and modern quotes to prove that sharp wit never goes out of fashion.

'Last week I stated that this was the ugliest woman I
had ever seen. I have since been visited by her sister and
now wish to withdraw that statement.' ~ Mark Twain

Classic Quotes

I've had a perfectly wonderful evening. But this wasn't it.

~ Groucho Marx

He has no enemies, but is intensely disliked by his friends.

~ Oscar Wilde

She wears her clothes as if they had been thrown on by a pitchfork.

~ Jonathan Swift

George Bernard Shaw invited Winston Churchill to the first night of a new play, ending with 'Bring a friend, if you have one.' Churchill wrote back: 'Impossible to be present for the first performance. Will attend the second – if there is one.'

If you want to know what God thinks of money – just look at the people he gave it to.

~ Dorothy Parker

A vacuum with nipples.

~ Otto Preminger, US film director (on Marilyn Monroe)

You have delighted us long enough.

~ Jane Austen

Sir. Your book is both good and original. Unfortunately, the parts that are good are not original, and the parts that are original are not good.

~ Anon

Such is the human race. Often it does seem a pity that Noah and his party didn't miss the boat.

~ Mark Twain

He is one of those people who would be enormously improved by death.

~ H. H. Munro

She looks like something that would eat its young.

~ Dorothy Parker
(on Dame Edith Evans)

The more I read him, the less I wonder that they poisoned him.

~ 19th century scholar Thomas Macauley (on Socrates)

Sir Stafford has a brilliant mind, until it is made up.

~ Lady Violet Bonham Carter
(on Labour Politician Sir Stafford Cripps)

I never desire to converse with a man who has written more than he has read.

~ Jonathan Swift's refusal to meet author Hugh Kelly

Modern Celebrity Quotes

You are quite sharp. It's just that in the purest sense of the word, you're ignorant.

~ **Richard Madeley, to Jade Goody**

Steve Martin has basically one joke and he's it.

~ **Dave Felton, Guitarist**

If David Seaman's dad had worn a condom, we'd still be in the World Cup.

~ **Nick Hancock, comedian**

'Why are you so fat?'
'Because every time I f*** your wife, she gives me a biscuit.'

~ **Legendary exchange between Glenn McGrath and the well-built Zimbabwean cricketer Eddo Brandes**

Arnold Schwarzenegger looks like a condom full of walnuts.

~ Clive James

All British have plain names, and that works pretty well over there.

~ Paris Hilton

He looks like a dwarf who's been dipped in a bucket of pubic hair.

~ Boy George (about Prince)

Boy George is all England needs – another queen who can't dress.

~ Joan Rivers

The face to launch a thousand dredgers.

~ Jack de Manio, British broadcaster (on Glenda Jackson)

Is Elizabeth Taylor fat? Her favourite food is seconds.

~ Joan Rivers

You're really quite attractive, Anne. In a Mr Burns from 'The Simpsons' kind of way.

~ Matt Blaize 'flirting' with Anne Robinson in a 'Weakest Link' special for new comics

I look at my friendship with her as like having a gall stone. You deal with it, there is pain, and then you pass it. That's all I have to say about Schmadonna.

~ Sandra Bernhard, about Madonna

I can't listen to that much Wagner. I start getting the urge to conquer Poland.

~ Woody Allen

Michael Jackson was a poor black boy who grew up to be a rich white woman.

~ Molly Ivins

They're So Mean They Get A Whole List

Mr Blackwell

In January every year, Mr Blackwell (ex-fashion designer and self-appointed acid-tongued critic) compiles a 'worst-dressed list' of celebrities he feels are worthy of note for their fashion crimes. Stating that 'elegance, classicism and restraint are never out of style and neither is a good 3-way mirror', here are some deemed to have failed the test:

47th List (2006)

Britney Spears and Paris Hilton: 'Two peas in an over-exposed pod'
Mariah Carey: 'Mariah the fashion pariah'
Meryl Streep: 'Mother of the bride'
Anna Nicole Smith: 'Queen Kong in cheap lingerie'
Camilla: 'The Duchess of Dowdy strikes again. In feathered hats that were once the rage, she resembles a petrified parakeet from the Jurassic age. A royal wreck'.

46th List (2005)

Britney: 'An over-the-hill Lolita'
Jessica Simpson: 'A cut-rate Rapunzel slingin' hash in a Vegas diner'
Renee Zellweger: 'A painted pumpkin on a pogo stick'

45th List (2004)

Sisters Jessica and Ashlee Simpson: 'These two prove that bad taste is positively genetic!'
Courtney Love: 'Medusa stuck in meltdown'
Paris Hilton: 'This is one Hilton that should be closed for renovation'

Ann Robinson – 'Weakest Link', US and UK shows

- This is a general-knowledge game, not a home for the bewildered.

- Aaron, you had a surprisingly good round. Was that a mistake?

- You're quite honestly the most stupid person I have ever met. Are you intelligent enough to be on the show?

- Let me say that the last round was a masterful display of memory loss and stupidity.

- He's completely West Ham

  (two stops short of Barking, on the London Underground)

- He has a bad balls-to-brains ratio.

Simon Cowell, X Factor USA and UK

- Simon: Are you taking singing lessons?
  Contestant: Yes sir!
  Simon: Well – get a good lawyer and sue your teacher.

- Simon: There are only so many words I can drag out of my vocabulary to describe how bad that was.

- Simon: You're called Champagne?
  Champagne: Yes Sir.
  Simon (referring to Champagne's net cloth on head): Well you look more like you work on a deli counter in that hat. Or in a poultry factory.

..... (Champagne sweats a bit, then sings)

- Simon: Mmmm – you call yourself 'Champagne', but that performance was more like cheap house wine.

..... (Champagne, refusing to leave, sings again)

- Simon: Champagne. You're flat!

- Simon (to elderly woman): Why have you come back
  again this year?
  Contestant: Well, I've got my teeth in this time and
  wanted to give it another go.
  Simon: But you managed to be even worse.
  Contestant: Up Yours.

- Simon: That performance was as relevant as a cat
  turning up for Crufts.

- Simon: It's a no I'm afraid.
  Contestant: But you could work with me – I need help.
  Simon: You need a help-line!

- Simon: I think it's time to disband.

- Contestant: Let me sing again.
  Simon (to contestant and family, who were crowding in):
  This girl cannot sing. You're not being fair to her
  leading her on in this way.
  Contestant: You've broken my heart. This was my
  dream.
  Simon: Well, the good news is, you found out today
  you're not going to be a singer, so now you're free
  to go and find another. Isn't that liberating!

- Contestant: Okay, so you hate me. Is there anything
  I can do to improve?
  Simon: Leave?

- Simon: God, so this is the best Minneapolis has to
  offer!
  Randy: Minni-hopeless.

She's spherical, like a globe. I could find out countries in her.

– The Comedy of Errors

A stuffed cloak-bag of guts. Swoln parcel of dropsies.

– Henry IV, Part I, ii

You are as a candle, the better part burnt out.

– Henry IV, Part II, I, ii

Let's meet as little as we can.

~ As You Like It, III, ii

You are smelt above the moon.

~ Coriolanus, Vi

He has not so much brain as ear wax.

~ Troilus & Cressida, V, i

I do desire we may be better strangers.

~ As you like it, III,ii

It looks as if it was put in by an Indian.

~ Gesturing to old-fashioned fusebox in
a factory near Edinburgh, 1999

Are you still throwing spears at other tribes?

~ Comment aimed at tribal elder at
Tjapukai Aboriginal Park, 2002

Do you know they have eating dogs for the anorexic now?

~ Said to a blind woman with a guide dog

If it has got four legs and it is not a chair, if it has got two wings and it flies but is not an aeroplane, and if it swims and it is not a submarine, the Cantonese will eat it.

~ Said at a World Wildlife Fund meeting in 1986

You are a woman aren't you?

~ Kenya 1984, after accepting a gift from an indigenous woman

Deaf? If you are near there, no wonder you are deaf.

~ said to young deaf people in Cardiff 1999, referring to nearby school's welcoming steel band

ALL THE WORLD'S A STAGE

The pursuit of fame is nothing new, but beware. Put yourself up for scrutiny and this is what you could get...

'Two things should be cut – the second act and the child's throat.'
– Noel Coward

Film and Theatre Reviews

'Rainman' is Dustin Hoffman humping one note on a piano for two hours and eleven minutes.

~ Pauline Kael

'Santa Clause III' is the cinematic equivalent of tertiary syphilis.

~ BBC Radio 5Live cinema critic Mark Kermode

For a comedy, this really isn't a whole lot of fun. The script is by writer/director Marc Lawrence (of such gems as 'Two Weeks Notice', 'Miss Congeniality' and 'Forces Of Nature') - red flags, anyone?

~ Website review of 'Music & Lyrics'

I didn't like the play, but then I saw it under adverse conditions – the curtain was up.

– Groucho Marx

The Play 'Perfectly Scandalous' was one of those plays in which all of the actors, unfortunately, enunciated very clearly.

– Robert Benchly

She ran the whole gamut of emotions from A – B.

– Dorothy Parker, about Katharine Hepburn

George Bernard Shaw was enjoying rapturous applause on the opening night of 'Arms and the Man'. As the applause died down, one heckler shouted 'rubbish' Shaw shouted back: 'I agree with you, my friend, but who are we two against the hundreds here who think otherwise?'

– courtesy of Acid Drops

Noel Coward became very irritated with Dame Edith Evans, as she continually got her lines wrong.

Edith, he protested, "this is not good enough. You don't know your lines."

"It's ridiculous", she retorted, "because this morning I said them over and over to myself, and I knew them backwards."

"And that's how you're saying them now dear."

~ courtesy of Acid Drops by Kenneth Williams

She was so dramatic she stabbed the potatoes at dinner.

Rev Sydney Smith
(on Mrs Siddons, tragedian actress)

The play opened at 8.40 sharp and closed at 10.40 dull.

~ Review of opening night of a Broadway show
by Hey-wood Broun

Heckler Stoppers

This is a special category, as it takes a unique kind of person to be able to stand in front of several hundred people and keep them entertained, whilst dealing artlessly with the one or two that are hell-bent on making you look foolish. Enter the rehearsed ad-lib...

- Let me give you a bit of advice. Never enter a battle of wits unarmed.

- Isn't it always the way? You come out for a quiet chat and some twat builds a comedy club round you. Shut up!

- This man is depriving a village somewhere of an idiot.

- Oh dear. I was going to do an impression of a wanker, but you just beat me to it.

- Go and stand over by the wall – that's plastered as well.

- As an outsider, what do you think of the human race?

- Do you ever wonder what life would be like if you'd had enough oxygen at birth?

- Where's the heckler? Ah – over there. That lovely natural blonde lady who dyes her roots black.

- With a face like that I'm surprised you're shouting and drawing attention to it.

- Your whole purpose in life is to serve as a warning to others.

- Look mate – you've already got the spots, so why don't you just leave the club, stop spoiling it for everyone else, and go and get a job at McDonalds?

- Could I borrow your brain? I'm building an idiot.

- Do you still love nature, even though it failed you so badly?

- Yes, I still remember the embarrassment of being unable to hold my alcohol publicly.

- Save your breath, you'll need it later to blow up your girlfriend.

- You are so ugly that if you entered an ugly contest, they'd say "Sorry, no professionals allowed."

- Are they your own teeth or are you breaking them in for a donkey?

- I saw you in the toilets earlier... surgery can do amazing things these days, you know.

Say It In A Song

Real songs with real sentiment behind them. Imagine the horror of finding you're the inspiration behind one of these...

- You're The Reason Our Kids Are So Ugly

- Get Your Tongue Otta My Mouth, 'Cos I'm kissing You Goodbye

- Thank God and Greyhound She's Gone

- I Flushed You From The Toilets Of My Heart

- I Don't Know Whether To Kill Myself Or Go Bowling

- She Got The Gold Mine and I Got The Shaft

- I Wouldn't Take Her To A Dogfight 'Cos I'm Afraid She'd Win

- You Were Only A Splinter As I Slid Down The Bannister Of Life

- May The Bird Of Paradise Fly Up Your Nose

How Can I Miss You If You Won't Go Away?

49

Great sit-com and film lines

Wait, I just remembered something! You're boring, and my legs work.

> – David Spade, as Finch in 'Just Shoot Me'

At first I thought he was walking his dog. Then I realised it was his date.

> – Edith Massey, 'Polyester'

Monica: Hi.
Chandler: Hi. You are not gonna believe what I did today.
Monica: Well, clearly you didn't shower or shave.

> – 'Friends'

You have completed a downward curve to imbecility.

– Blackadder to Baldrick, 'Blackadder'

Lord Flasheart: 'I wasn't born yesterday, you know'
Edmund Blackadder: 'More's the pity, we could have started your personality from scratch.'

– 'Blackadder 4'

Neat? She was so anally retentive she couldn't sit down for fear of sucking up the furniture.

– Patsy, 'Absolutely Fabulous'

Get a haircut and a boiler suit so I don't have to keep explaining you to my friends.

– Edie to Saffy, 'Absolutely Fabulous'

Your hair looks snazzy... is that your mum's money coming through? All part of the bereavement dividend!

~ Alan to Lynn, 'I'm Alan Partridge'

Brian: I see it as a tribute to Christo, the artist.
Tim: I see it as a waste of Baco, the foil.

~ A comment on Daisy's party decorations, 'Spaced'

DID THEY REALLY SAY THAT?

We've all had those moments when we've sat there after being verbally smashed and grabbed, wondering if the person opposite really said what we thought they did. And more importantly, did they mean what we suspect they mean? It's an art form in itself!

Inadvertent put-downs

This was a real conversation with my friend. Totally cringy...

Me: Oh! What have you done to your hair? It looks like a wig.
Friend: Er, it is.
Me: Wow. Blimey! Amazing!! I'd never have guessed!

~ Sarah, Beaconsfield

I was eating a cream cake to celebrate a colleague's birthday, when my office manager walked past. We gestured to the cake but she just said "Oh – no thanks. I'd love to eat like you do, but I value my figure too much."

~ Tracey, Birmingham

My young son saw my backside and announced that it needed ironing. I have reversed out of every bedroom I've ever been in since.

~ Lou, New York

I was running across Russell Square in London, in pursuit of a bus, but was stopped in my tracks by a bag lady sitting on the floor, who felt it was her duty to shout after me: 'Oy – you need a sports bra!'

– Janet, Coleshill

I was attacked on the London underground by a group of girls. Figuring I had nothing to lose by a certain stage, I told one of them (the horrible fat one), that she hadn't got the legs to be wearing such a short skirt. She stopped attacking me and burst into tears. I guess that proves we've all got an achilles heel – thank God I found hers in time!

– Ruth, Birmingham

I'd had breast cancer, and made friends with some of the other women in the ward. You'd think at this horrible stage of life, you'd be treated with a bit of respect, but no. The poor woman in the bed next to me asked if she'd have enough flesh left for a reconstruction. Without batting an eyelid, the surgeon barked back, 'you've got enough in that stomach to reconstruct a whole ward'. Now that was insulting!

~ Justine, Birmingham

In Italy, they emphasise a point by exaggerating it. For example, one man, referring to a woman who did nothing but clean, said that she was 'doppiamente (twice over) a slave'.

So, applying this reasoning to his burgeoning language skills, my Italian boyfriend screamed at me during a row to 'fuck off five times'. I nearly died laughing.

~ Helen, Southport

Kindly Put Downs

When you don't want to be nasty, but you don't really want to lie either...

When one friend asked another to pass on his interest to a certain young lady, she naturally asked what he looked like. After a long pause, his mate described him as 'not really being ugly, but he has got quite 'agricultural' features.'

– Dave, Ashby

When asked what it was like working with Julie Andrews, the Canadian actor Christopher Plummer replied that it was 'like being hit over the head with a Valentine's card'.

– Dictionary of Insulting Quotations

My grandchild advised us not to buy a hot tub, as he'd seen how wrinkled it made his parents when they stayed in for long periods, and 'seeing as you've got so many already, it would be a waste of money'.

– Penny B, Bournemouth

THE WORD ON THE STREET

Modern times call for modern methods. Gone are the days of graceful taunts and witty parlour vitriol as ladies attended their samplers and sipped tea. No – all that's gone, so bring on the night club toilets, websites and strip clubs. Oh lordy!

foundation will definitely help madam. Your pores aren't too open - they're more ajar.

Overheard Put Downs and Insults

Come on in gents. We've got 100 girls, and only two of them are ugly.

~ Outside a Vancouver strip club

Girl One: Did you see Emma with that f***king dress up round her f**king waist?
Girl Two: (applying mascara). Yeah – I just hope he bought her dinner first.

~ Nightclub toilet in Birmingham

... and now she's got an open-top sports car, so she can feel the wind in her facial hair...

~ Toilets in department store, two bitchy girls talking

Nice effort luv. Have you been deaf for long?

~ Overheard as girl left stage after
doing karaoke in a pub

Well she was very average. Not the most graceful dancer. When she was en-pointe with her leg out, she looked like a dog at a lampost.

~ Overheard upon leaving the theatre, after a ballet

... and kissing him, his lips were like wet liver... it would never have worked – he even looked scruffy undressed....

~ Girls' night out, discussing men

And you girl. What exactly are you?
I'm springtime miss.
Springtime? Springtime? You look more like a bursting sofa full of mould.' Springtime indeed!

~ At local dance exams, Chief examiner
(referring to girl of around 12, dressed in green leotard,
green tights with swathes of green fabric hanging off her)

Website Rancour

Chatroom Insults

You are proper fit. Just like a butcher's dog. With the emphasis firmly on dog.

~ www.chavscum.co.uk

Wasn't he the one in East 17? The one on the right. Wasn't he the result of a genetic experirment(sic)? Mating John Merrick and Ann Widdecombe.

~ www.chavscum.co.uk
(Re: a picture posted on the site)

You are all just fucktards.

~ one chav's response to his critics on
www.chavspotting.co.uk

Vitriolic Voices

If you fancy a whine – what better place than online? Here are some of the best:

American Express (AmeXsuX.com / Amexsucks.com)

- Amex – Do leave home without it.

- What the hell is wrong with this company? Does satan work there? Are the company picnics held in Auschwitz for the sentimental value? They are all liars and scroundrels with no interest in actually doing what they say.

The British Airways Visa card (on E-pinions.com)

- Posted comment: 'The Official Credit Card of the Marquis du Sade' (Jul 10 2001 (Updated Jan 08 '07)

Under the ' You were never Fuglier' section

Nancy Dell'Olio

- Nancy: "I am not 46 – I am 43. I am fabulous anyway – I look 20 years younger."
  Writer: "I want the same mirror this mad cow uses"!

'Invasion Of The Zombie Hands' (featuring Nicole Ritchie, Posh, Nicole Kidman)

- Writer says: 'Get some collagen injected, buy some damn gloves. Better yet try eating something and putting some damn meat on your bony old claws'.

Barbra Streisand

• Re: picture of Barbra in a see-through dress revealing no bra and droopy puppies.
  Writer says: 'Good grief! What on earth was Mental Yentl thinking?'!

Russell Crowe (on Fametracker.com)

• For those of you unfamiliar with the nuances of Hollywood euphemisms, the word 'perfectionist' can be translated roughly as 'unrepentant asshole'. The word 'driven' can be translated roughly as 'obstinate prick'...

AFTER THE LOVE HAS GONE

Unless you're very lucky in love, the chances are that eventually sweet nothings will be replaced with sweet F.A. Here are some of the more printable submissions we offer up as proof.

Dating Insults

A guy I was dating called me a huge fat pig. Although I was hurt, I managed to turn it around by saying, 'Sir. I suggest if you want me on all fours and squealing, you talk nicer to me than that!'

~ Sue, Birmingham

I think it was a thinly-disguised insult when a new boyfriend said I 'smelt like a vegetarian'...

~ Nicky, Poole

I was very insulted when my husband asked me to stay quiet during sex, 'or pretend to be Jackie' (my best mate).

~ Petra, Los Angeles

I turned up for a date feeling very glamorous with my new, fashionable look (cut off trousers, peasant top with full sleeves and a hippy-type headband), but the wind was taken out of my sails when my date exclaimed, 'My God! Who got you ready?'

– Lara, Birmingham

I was showing my partner some pictures of myself a few years before we met. He visibly perked up, going 'Cor – you were a cracker back then'.

– Sally, Bristol

I was making love with my partner, when he stopped and asked me to stand in front of the mirror. Thinking we were in for a bit of kinkiness, I eagerly obliged. Then he said, 'I thought you'd put on weight. Just look at your tummy from the side.'

My confidence fell right through the floor, and hasn't really ever recovered.

– J.P., Birmingham

Parting Shots

When my boyfriend finished with me, his cruel, horrible parting shot was referring to my latest intimate waxing (I'd gone for the 'landing strip' look). He told me he preferred a woman much more natural, and ended by saying 'it made me sick. Every time I looked at you, I was reminded of a threadbare hall carpet'.

— Kelly, Wales

I was trying to be a better partner, and decided to visit a life coach. After a while, it became apparent that my girlfriend wasn't impressed. Her last line, that still rings in my ears was 'and all you ever thought about was sex. And let me tell you – a hard-on does not count as personal growth!'

— Mikey, Vancouver

One of the most horrible things ever, was a boyfriend looking back over his shoulder as he walked away for the last time, saying 'And by the way – you look really ugly when you're asleep'. How cruel is that?

– Anon, Yorkshire

My boyfriend finished with me saying I was 'too much of a handful', to which I replied, 'Fine. Just wish I could have said the same to you'.

– Claire, Hounslow

My boyfriend thought he'd really hurt me when I finished with him by shouting after me, '...and I was shagging your best mate all the time anyway.'

But I got the upper hand by shouting back the truth, '...well so was I!' That shut him up.

– Kelly, Rotherham

SCHOOL DAZE

These stories come from the days it was considered 'encouraging' to be brutally honest. They were also the days when you could hit children, call them idiots and expect them to leave as rounded individuals. Read on with a pinch of salt...

Report

Tim would do so much better if he did not regard chemistry as a branch of magic!

School Reports of The Famous

(with thanks to 'Could Do Better' by Catherine Hurley – Simon & Schuster)

The man is every inch a fool, but luckily for him he's not very tall.

– **Norman Wisdom, Comic**

It would seem that Briers thinks he is running the school and not me. If this attitude persists one of us will have to leave.

– **Richard Briers, Actor**

He is no longer such a contented dweller in Philistia.

– **Lord Longford**

He shows great originality, which must be curbed at all costs.

– Sir Peter Ustinov

Though her written work is the product of an obviously lively imagination, it is a pity that her spelling derives from the same source.

– Beryl Bainbridge, Novelist

School Reports of the Non-Famous

Ruth is a keen typist, who has currently attained a speed of 35 mistakes a minute.

~ Writer's first year secretarial college report

With regards to the violin, Jenny has an ear for music. However, to accompany it she still needs the fingering, the timing, the bowing technique and the patience.

~ Jenny Worrall, Portsmouth
(now a housewife who still loves classical music)

An evenly-balanced child is a rarity, thus it is a joy to teach Keith, as the chip is firmly on both of his shoulders

~ Keith R, Somerset
(Keith grew up and went into politics, by the way)

Patricia has achieved the rare honour of taking a full term to learn to thread her sewing machine. Unfortunately, by the time she had made her garment to its original specifications, she had grown out of it. A great disappointment all round.

~ **Patricia Green, London** (who has never sewn since)

An utter idiot who will amount to nothing. This boy can only ever aspire to the heady heights of becoming a has-been

~ **Andrew Fuller, Birmingham** (X Factor reject and sales rep)

After four testing years as Brian's form tutor, he is now ready to leave school and take his place in the world. I would therefore like to give him a leaving gift. However, he must promise to fulfil his part of the bargain.

~ **Brian Bramwell, London** (unemployed)

It is only with the improvement in Stephen's handwriting, that the full horror of his spelling has become apparent.

Steve D, London (now a speechwriter)

THE WORLD OF WORK

Everyone has applied for a job they wanted and not got it. Here are some of the most heart-warming rejections to prove you're not the only one getting it wrong.

Applications and rejections

I auditioned for the musical 'Cats' back when it was a new production. Unfortunately, I turned up at the dance auditions by mistake (I'm a singer), but I figured, seeing as I was there, I might as well have a go. I had to borrow everything to wear and looked dreadful, so was really nervous when I got on stage to see Andrew Lloyd Webber in the front row, along with the choreographer etc.

I got through the first 'cut' of dancers, but in the second round, I moved in the opposite direction from everyone else, and managed to send somebody literally flying over me and onto the floor. There was a terrible silence, then the choreographer screamed 'You. You in the pink and purple'. I looked around, and then said 'Who? Me?' He wagged his finger and shrieked 'Yes. You. The one dressed as a pimple that's about to burst. Just leave the stage to the professionals.' There was a gasp of horror, a small ripple of agreement and I slinked off, feeling utterly mortified.

~ Cassie, Isle of Wight

I went for a job interview once, where this guy ran an agency that represented high-profile celebs and film stars. He was a nightmare and behaved like a prima-donna through the whole interview, saying my duties would include 'getting my morning bagel, overseeing my diary, collecting my cleaning and taking Trixie (the dog) out and picking up after her.' Rather annoyed at the waste of time, I pointed out that the job advert hadn't suggested any of this. He retorted by saying 'well obviously, you haven't got the qualities I'm looking for'. I responded that, perhaps, the advert would have been better worded just saying 'Wanker Needs Doormat'! His face, as I left, was a picture.

~ Sophie, Holland Park

An unattractive young man with indistinct speaking voice and extremely unfortunate appearance.

~ alleged BBC rejection of Tommy Cooper

Fred Astaire – can't act, can't sing can dance a little.

~ RKO pictures screen test report

I'd just had a job interview that had gone well. Five minutes after leaving the office, I unfortunately bumped into my prospective boss again as I waited by the elevator. I was waiting to leave, and he was passing, now obviously on his way to the bathroom. He carried on walking past, but said goodbye and all the best to me, once more. Buoyed up with confidence at how well things had gone, I shouted after him in my best jock/college-boy, new buddy voice – 'cheers Andrew. And don't forget. More than two shakes is a wank!' God – I don't know what possessed me. I saw his shoulders stiffen, his stride change just for a nanosecond, and I knew I'd blown it. The rejection letter was a classic, saying that he was 'thankful for the opportunity to put right what could possibly have been the most grave mistake in the company's history'. Nice eh?

– Paul, Toronto

Another day of commerce

I'm an air steward, so we come in for a lot of flack in a normal day. One such day was brightened considerably, when a very drunk man was attempting to persuade the ground-staff to let him board. He waved his ticket in the girl's face, and getting redder and redder, he shouted, "But I'm a first-class passenger." To which she calmly replied, "No sir. You're a passenger with a first-class ticket."

~ George M. (British Airways), Staffordshire

After-dinner speaker just about to start his talk at the Savoy.
'Can everybody hear me?'
Weary voice from the back replies: 'I can hear you perfectly, but I'm willing to change with anyone who can't.'

~ from Acid Drops

I used to teach in China, and in the class I inherited, all my students had adopted English names (although I'm not sure Dwayne, Twinkle or Silo were great choices). Anyway – they gave me this lovely sounding name, which they insisted 'kind of means sun-kissed coral, miss'. Yeah – right. I got a clue they were lying because whenever somebody asked me my Chinese name and I repeated it, they'd collapse laughing.

The worst one was in a bar when I was with some businessmen. The hostess there asked my name, and laughed so much, and so loudly that it was embarrassing. Anyway – an honest friend took me on one side and confided that, thanks to my love of wearing shorts, these ******* students had given me a name that actually translated into 'Old English with wobbly fat thighs'.

I was furious, but I got my own back by not letting on that I'd sussed out. So, I simply taught them an English traditional song, that, I informed them, was sung everywhere in England, including weddings, christenings and especially at funerals. I told them that it was traditional to start the singing whenever it seemed the occasion had flagged, or things had gone quiet, and it was the honoured responsibility of the visitor to start the singing, and everyone would join in. Thus, it was with great satisfaction, that I sent a whole group of students out into the world, heavily coached and primed to sing the Goon's Ying-Tong song at the first available opportunity.

– Anna Smith, Gloucester

As a trainee ad executive, I always tried really hard to add value to any meeting I was in. However, I realised it was pointless, when I shouted out my brilliant new idea one day, and my manager shot me down with 'You have two ears, and one mouth Stephen. Use them in that ratio.'

– Steve D, London

There was a huge strike at our workplace, and I was called in to give my recommendations. There was one really difficult shop steward, and I was asked what we should do about him. In my report, I simply wrote that he should be 'fired with enthusiasm'. He knew it had a double meaning, and so did I, but nobody could pin anything on me.

– Peter Blake, Birmingham

Military intelligence is a contradiction in terms.

Groucho Marx

Abraham Lincoln was at his wittiest when he wrote the following letter to one of his procrastinating generals:
'My dear McClellan.
If you don't want to use the army, I should like to borrow it for a while.

Yours respectfully
A. Lincoln

~ **from Acid Drops**

LOVE THY NEIGHBOUR

Forget big melting pots and all being the same under the skin! If we can't get on with our own families, there's little chance of getting on with people across the pond. Here's what various parts of the world think of their 'brothers and sisters'!

'Few things can be less tempting or more dangerous than a Greek woman over the age of thirty.' – John Carne

Americans

We Americans suffer from an enforced ignorance. We don't know about anything that's happening outside our country. Our stupidity is embarrassing.

~ Michael Moore, about his own country

The trouble with America is that there are far too many wide open spaces surrounded by teeth.

~ Charles Luckman, US writer

Too many Americans are looked upon as dollar chasers. This is a cruel libel, even if it is reiterated thoughtlessly by the Americans themselves.

~ Albert Einstein

Nothing is wrong with California that a rise in the ocean level wouldn't cure.

– Ross MacDonald (1915–1983)

You Gotta Live Somewhere.

– Suggested motto for Cleveland

Of course, America had often been discovered before Columbus, but it had always been hushed up.

– Oscar Wilde

No-one ever went broke underestimating the taste of the American public.

– HL Mencken

And the rest...

Germans are flummoxed by humor, the Swiss have no concept of fun, the Spanish think there is nothing at all ridiculous about eating dinner at midnight, and the Italians should never, ever have been let in on the invention of the motor car.

~ Bill Bryson

Continental people have a sex life; the English have hot-water bottles.

~ George Mikes, Hungarian writer, 'How To Be an Alien', 1946

The Englishman is never content but when he is grumbling.

~ Scottish saying

The Irish gave the bagpipes to the Scots as a joke, but the Scots haven't seen the joke yet.

~ Oliver Herford

The Japanese have perfected good manners and made them indistinguishable from rudeness.

~ Paul Theroux

Since both its national products, snow and chocolate, melt, the cuckoo clock was invented solely in order to give tourists something solid to remember it by.

~ Alan Coren, humourist, on Switzerland

A cricket tour in Australia would be the most delightful period in your life... if you were deaf.

~ Harold Larwood, English Cricketer

All Australians are an uneducated and unruly mob.

~ Douglas Jardine

He waddles like an Armenian bride.

~ Osmanli saying

The friendship of the French is like their wine, exquisite but of short duration.

~ German saying

A Turk who hears the word 'paradise' asks "Is there any gold to be looted there?"

~ Persian saying

The only thing [the British] have ever given European farming is mad cow. You can't trust people who cook as badly as that. After Finland, it's the country with the worst food.

~ Jacques Chirac,
during the bidding process for the 2012 Olympics

Do not trust a Hungarian unless he has a third eye in his forehead.

~ Czech saying

Trust a Brahman before a snake, and a snake before a harlot, and a harlot before an Afghan.

~ Hindu saying

Marry a German and you'll see that the woman have hairy tongues.

~ Rumanian saying

He is as grateful as a German.

~ Polish saying

The Bavarian will not budge before you walk on him.

~ German saying

The Scotchman is one who keeps the Sabbath and every other thing he can lay his hands on.

~ American saying

POLITICAL INSULTS

Plato said that the penalty for not being in politics is that you end up being governed by your inferiors. Imagine how heartened he'd be to know that absolutely nothing has changed.

'George Bush – big hat. No cattle.'
– Ann Richards

George W Bush

I would like to apologize for referring to George W. Bush as a 'deserter.' What I meant to say is that George W. Bush is a deserter, an election thief, a drunk driver, a WMD liar and a functional illiterate. And he poops his pants.

~ Filmmaker Michael Moore

Did the training wheels fall off?

~ Senator John Kerry, after being told by reporters that President Bush took a tumble during a bike ride

Big hat, no cattle

~ Former Governor of Texas, Ann Richards

Poor George, he can't help it... He was born with a silver foot in his mouth.

~ Ann Richards

General

If life were fair, Dan Quayle would be making a living asking, "Do you want fries with that?"

– John Cleese

You get fifteen democrats in a room, and you get twenty opinions.

– Senator Patrick Leahy

He is racist, he's homophobic, he's xenophobic and he's a sexist. He's the perfect Republican candidate.

– Bill Press
(on Pat Buchanan)

What makes him think a middle aged actor, who's played with a chimp, could have a future in politics?

– Ronald Reagan on Clint Eastwood's bid to become mayor of Carmel

Winston has devoted the best years of his life to preparing his impromptu speeches.

– F. E. Smith (1872–1930) on Winston Churchill (1874–1965)

Attila the Hen.

– Clement Freud on Margaret Thatcher

Don't be so humble – you are not that great.

– Golda Meir (1898–1978) to a visiting diplomat

The labour Party has lost the last four elections. If they lose another, they get to keep the liberal party.

– Clive Anderson

You don't reach Downing Street by pretending you've travelled the road to Damascus when you haven't even left home.

– Margaret Thatcher on Neil Kinnock

THE A - Z OF PUT-DOWNS

Ageing
- (to older person) Was it cold in the ground this morning?
- You're so old your first job was as Cain and Abel's babysitter.
- Does Jurassic Park bring back fond memories?

Arse
- He had a backside that was so big, people would jog around him for exercise.
- She had an arse like two open barn doors
- Do stunt agencies hire you as an air mattress?

Attraction
- They do say that opposites attract, so I hope it's not long before you find yourself someone clever, cultured and witty.
- What am I? Flypaper for freaks?
- The only thing you'll ever attract is gravity.

Bitchy

- Do you know what would make you look really good? Distance.
- Girl 1: Why aren't you married yet?
  Girl 2: Why aren't you thin?
- That's a lovely dress. It's just a shame your body doesn't suit it.

Blonde

- What's a blonde's favourite nursery rhyme? Hump me, dump me.
- Why should blondes not have coffee breaks at work? Because it takes too long to re-train them.
- Heard about the blonde who spent 20 minutes staring at an orange juice carton because it said 'concentrate'!

Boring

- You are so boring you couldn't even entertain a doubt.
- She's so boring you fall asleep halfway through her name.
- His clothes are more entertaining than he is.

Clothing
- Does she drink and dress?
- Look at the clothes – is there a potting shed nearby?
- I've seen wounds better dressed than you

Common Sense
- You've just proved that the funny thing about common sense is it ain't that common.
- There has been an alarming increase in the number of things you know nothing about.
- Common sense would say that alphabet soup is probably wasted on you.

Compliments
- Moonlight becomes you. Darkness even more!
- Lovely suit. When did the clown die?
- Nice perfume – did you plan to marinade in it?

Dance

- You got me on the dance floor by saying dancing was in your blood. If that's the case, I take it your circulation has now stopped?
- You only chose to be a ballerina so no-one would tell you off for having too much attitude.
- You might think you're a ballerina, but that performance was more like Swine Lake!

Dating

- Man: Can I buy you a drink?
  Woman: Can't I just have the money?
- There's no way I'm your type – I'm not inflatable.
- Sorry – I don't date outside of my species.

Dense

- He's so dense, light bends round him.
- You're so thick you couldn't pour water out of a boot even with instructions on the heel.
- Her brain is as busy as a hog farmer in Israel.

Education

- Education and intelligence are not the same thing.
- He doesn't know the meaning of the word fear. But then again, he doesn't know the meaning of most words.
- You are very educated in maths. You add trouble, subtract pleasure, divide attention and multiply ignorance.

Enquiries

- What would you say was my best feature? (Answer) Your ornamental pond!
- Is your birth certificate an apology from the condom factory?
- After they made you and broke the mould, did they beat up the mould maker?

Exaggerate

- Stop exaggerating. I've got Deja moo - as in I've heard all this bull before.
- When you said in your profile that you had the face of a saint, you weren't exaggerating. Too bad it's the face of a Saint Bernard!

Face
- Last time I saw a face like that, it had a jockey on it.
- Her face was her chaperone.
- That's what happens when cousins marry.

Fat
- He's so fat, his blood type is Ragu.
- She's so fat she had to have her ears pierced so the family could see the tv.
- You know you're fat when you're diagnosed with a flesh-eating virus, but are still given 22 years to live.

Frigid
- She's so frigid, she smears anti-climb paint on her stockings.
- She's so frigid, her water bed turned to ice.
- It's been so long since there was any action, she no longer passes water – she passes dust!

Genitals

- I'm not saying you're small in that department, but it barely parted my hairs!
- I've always wanted to bring out the animal in my lovers. What a shame I've just met your inner hamster.
- I think you're mistaking me for a computer. I'm not built to take a 3" floppy.

Glasses

- Are those glasses, or have you just got a job as a welder?
- Did you get such thick glasses to reflect your brain, or to help see further into your future?

Gloat

- The good thing about all your mistakes is the joy it brings to others.
- I can't argue with your stupidity. First you'll bring me down to your level, then you'll beat me with experience.
- Good luck in court. After all – your fate is in the hands of people who weren't smart enough to get out of jury service.

Hair

- He is so hairy he wasn't born – he was trapped.
- Next time you shave could you stand a little closer to the razor?
- His mother was so hairy, she had to breast feed him through a straw.

Hatred

- I've had many cases of love that were just infatuation, but this hatred I feel for you is the real thing.
- Why don't you slip into something more comfortable. Like a coma.
- The world is divided into those who leave their mark, and others, like you, who leave their stain.

Health

- You must constantly suffer from laryngitis as you're such a pain in the neck.
- What a shame you spent so much time getting rid of the halitosis, only to find nobody liked you anyway.
- Laughter is the best medicine, so get a mirror and stay healthy.

Informed
- He's so badly informed he thinks Dom Perignon is a mafia boss.
- She's so badly informed she thinks chlamydia is a village in Wales.
- I'd like to be as informed as you, but there's no chance I could ever get my head that high up my backside.

Instructions
- Just because you have one, don't behave like one.
- Don't go to a mind-reader, go to a palmist. I know you've got a palm.
- Earth is full. Go home.

Intellect
- What's on your mind? If you'll forgive the over-statement.
- His IQ is the reason they had to invent negative numbers
- If his IQ was two points higher, he'd be a rock.

Jerks
- How come every jerk knows the least, but knows it the loudest?
- April 1st must feel like such a comfortable day for you.
- I heard you used up all your sick days, so you called in dead?

Jumped-up
- You're a pretentious fool who has delusions of adequacy.

Jury
- The jury's out and they find you guilty of being so ugly you'd make a freight train take a dirt road.
- Never trust a jury. Reaching a conclusion simply means they got tired of thinking.

Killjoy
- You have the ability to take the joy from any situation, and leave me feeling more helpless than the owner of a sick goldfish.
- Psychiatrists are such killjoys – the type of men who'd go to a strip club and watch the audience.
- If you heard opportunity knock, you'd ask it to keep the noise down.

Knowledgeable
- After meeting you, I know for sure that celibacy is the new black.
- People like you who think you know everything, are very annoying to those of us who actually do.
- You are a font of knowledge – with a huge leak.

Looks

- When you were born, did the midwife slap your mother?
- She was so hideous that when she went to the fairground, the haunted house offered her a job.
- That's what they mean by dark and handsome. When it's dark – he's handsome.

Loser

- Your DNA must cry itself to sleep at night.
- The overwhelming power of the sex drive was demonstrated by the fact that someone was willing to father him.
- Some drink from the fountain of knowledge – you only gargled.

Make-up
- Nice make up. Let's hit it with a bat and see if candy comes out.
- Whatever look you were going for – you missed!
- And you say you've been for a makeover? You certainly were.

Marriage
- She would have been married, but she lifted the veil too soon.
- She's had three husbands. One of her own, and two of somebody elses'.
- In Hollywood, a marriage is a success if it outlasts milk. – Rita Rudner

Mothers
- Your mother's so hairy you must have got rugburn on the way out!
- Your mother's so nasty that when I called to say hi, I got an ear infection.
- My mother never saw the irony in calling me a son-of-a-bitch.

Narrowminded
- He was so narrowminded he could see through a keyhole with both eyes.
- You are so narrowminded that when you walk your earrings knock together.
- I don't know what makes you so narrowminded, but it really works.

Nauseating
- The best bit of you was the bit that ran down your mother's leg.
- When he was born, the doctors waited for the garlic bread to be delivered with him.
- Slit your wrists – it will lower your blood pressure.

Numbskull
- You're so dumb you need a cue card to say 'huh?'
- You are an experiment in artificial stupidity.
- He has an IQ of 2, and it takes 3 to grunt.

Observations
- People wrapped up in themselves make very small packages
- It's hard to get the big picture, when you have such a small screen
- You'll never make a comeback as you've never been anywhere.

Opinions
- I have opinions of my own – strong opinions – but I don't always agree with them. (George Bush)
- When I want your opinion, I'll give it to you.
- I never know what I think about something until I read what I've written on it. (William Faulkner)

Orthodontics
- Do you mind if I sit back a little? Because your breath is very bad. (Said to Larry King from Donald Trump)
- You have teeth the druids could use as a place of worship.
- Your teeth are so yellow you could spit butter.

Parents

- His father was a boxer. And his mother, a dalmation.
- His dad was so dirty, he thought hygiene was a feelgood American musical.
- He gets it all from his father – tall, dark and obnoxious.

Personality

- He had the personality of a telephone dialling tone.
- What a great party. Later on we'll get some fluid and embalm each other. (Neil Simon)
- If she moved any less, they'd draw a chalk line around her.

Politics

- How can you tell when a planeload of politicians has landed? The engine goes off, but the whining carries on.
- Democracy is the worst form of Government except all those other forms that have been tried. (Winston Churchill)
- A politician should never let their mind wander – it's too little to be left alone.

Quandaries

- How do you keep an idiot busy for hours? Give him piece of paper with 'Please Turn Over' written on both sides.
- I just can't work it out. Usually someone with a face of such limited appeal makes up for it with a sparkling personality...
- It must be such a quandary, choosing between being accepted as you are, or being liked.

Queries

- And which dwarf are you?
- Do you step on rakes for a living?
- How's your horse? What horse? The one that kicked you in the face.

Quotes

- I have more talent in my smallest fart than you have in your entire body. (Walter Matthau, to Barbra Streisand)
- I loathe you. You revolt me stewing in your consumption... you are a loathsome reptile – I hope you die. (D. H. Lawrence, to Katherine Mansfield)
- She's like an apple turnover that got crushed in a grocery bag on a hot day. (Camille Paglia, about Drew Barrymore)

Reincarnation

- You make me believe in reincarnation. Nobody could be as stupid as you in just one lifetime.
- Each time round, we're supposed to live and learn. You just live.
- Perhaps the whole purpose of coming back again was to serve as a warning to others.

Relationships

- Women might be able to fake orgasms. But men can fake a whole relationship. (Sharon Stone)
- Save your breath – you'll need it later for your date.
- You'll make some man really happy one day. Then he'll zip up his pants, leave £10 on the dresser and be gone...

Retorts

- Is that a gun in your pocket, or are you just pleased to see me? (Answer). No, it's a gun.
- Please – keep talking. I always yawn when I'm interested.
- I've only got one nerve left, and you're getting on it.

Sarcastic

- Do I look like a fucking people person?
- Sarcasm is just one more service we offer.
- If I throw a stick, will you leave?

Sex

- She's a lot like train tracks – she's been laid across the country.
- His technique was a bit like dining in a canteen. I lay back, he served himself.
- Man: I badly want to make love to you.
  Woman: You've already done that

Shallow

- Of course you're not shallow. It's perfectly normal to fall out of love with someone if their yacht sinks.
- You're shallower than a kids' paddling pool
- Mercedez Benz – a mechanical device that increases sexual arousal in certain women.

Talent
- Don't feel bad honey – a lot of people have no talent.
- Is there no beginning to your talent?
- Your DNA is a talent-free zone.

Telephone
- Please do give me a call. It would give me great pleasure to hang up on you.
- If you ever need me, please hesitate to call.
- That's odd. You sounded handsome on the phone.

Trailer Trash
- You must be trailer trash. The ceiling fan is 6' high and it still ruined your hair-do.
- If a woman is out of your league, it just means she bowls on a different night.
- You must be trailer trash. You've been married three times and still have the same in-laws.

Ugly
- You owe me a drink. You're so shocking, that I dropped my glass when I saw you.
- You're so ugly, I bet they had to tint the windows on your incubator.
- He was that ugly he had to trick or treat over the phone.

Underwear
- Man: Why wear a bra? You've nothing to put in it.
  Woman: Well, you wear trousers don't you.

Unpleasant
- Her body wasn't so much a temple, as an amusement park.
- Oh my God – look at you! Anyone else hurt in the accident?
- I don't want you to turn the other cheek – it's just as ugly.

Vamp
- Brassy, brazen witch on a mortgaged broomstick, a steamroller with cleats. – Walter Kerr, on Ethel Merman
- There goes the good time that was had by all – Bette Davis

Vanity
- He's the type of man who will end up dying in his own arms. (Mamie Van Doren, about Warren Beatty)
- He's so conceited his eyes behold each other perfectly.

Vitriol
- When should I phone you? (Answer) Whenever I'm not there.
- I'd rather stay in and self-harm than have a date with you.
- If I lend you £20 and never see you again, it will have been worth it.

Weight

- She had thighs by Ben & Jerry.
- She dresses well – I think the label is 'House of Lard'.
- Your weight issue was definitely highlighted by the fact they installed speed bumps at the running buffet.

Wishes

- I wish I could bump into you again. Preferably when you're walking and I'm driving.
- You have a lot of well wishers. They would all like to throw you down one.
- I wish you were a statue and I was a pigeon.

Work

- No. Just because no-one understands what you do, it doesn't mean you're an artist!
- You must have a low opinion of your workmates if you think they're your equals.
- Would you like to replace my business partner who died this morning? I'll arrange it with the undertaker.

Xenophobia

- The great thing about Glasgow now is that if there is a nuclear attack it'll look exactly the same afterwards. (Billy Connolly)
- Each section of the British Isles has it's own way of laughing, except the Wales, which doesn't. (Stephen Leacock)

X-Ray

- The radiologist x-rayed your brain today. It turned out to be quite a vacation for them.
- I was so delighted when the x-ray showed a hole in your heart. Too bad it turned out to be a Polo mint in your top pocket.

Youth

- Can I spend the evening with you?
  (Answer) – I gave up babysitting years ago.
- Where have you been all my life.
  (Answer) – What do you mean? I wasn't born for the first half of it.

Zip

- She wouldn't harm a fly. Unless it was open.

Zit

- I've kept my youthful complexion.
  (Answer) So I see – all the spots of a 13 year-old!
- You're so zitty that if you threw a boomerang, it would make a bit for freedom.

Zodiac

- Man: What's Your Sign? Woman: 'Keep Away'
- It says you are going to leave a permanent impression on someone this month. Better cover up your warts.
- Now I know the sign you were born under – 'red light district'!

INTERNATIONAL INSULTS

Isn't culture amazing...

Amharic

- *Timbatam.*
  Rotten Stinky.

- *Vay vay doo boos wok.*
  You worship my shit.

- *Keffafi.*
  Fuck-Face.

Brazilian

- *Vai peidar na água pra ver se sai bolhinhas.*
  Go to fart in water and make bubbles.

- *Você é burro de dar dó.*
  You're so stupid, people pity you.

- *Cheira meu saco.*
  Smell my bollocks.

- *Do jeito que você é feio, seria melhor barbear a bunda e andar de costas.*
  You're so ugly you should shave your ass and walk backwards.

- *O cu da sua mãe é tão grande que um trem do metrô poderia passar nele sem problemas.*
  Your mom's ass is so big that a subway train could pass through it with no problems.

- *Senta em cima e brinca de elevador.*
  Sit on it and pretend it's an elevator.
  (used as a comeback if someone shows you the finger)

Bulgarian

- *Pederas grozen gyrbaw prokazhen.*
  Unsightly hunchbacked leper queer.

- *Grozna si kato salata.*
  You're as ugly as a salad.

- *Nosa ti e kato ruska putka.*
  Your nose is like a Russian pussy.

- *Tolko si debel che edinstvenite ti snimki sa satelitni.*
  You are so fat that all you're pictures are from satellite.

- *Slon da ti go turne v mirizlivia guz.*
  Let an elephant fuck you in your smelly ass.

Danish

- *Sut mine rådne løg.*
  Suck my hairy onions.

- *Hun er så fed, at man må rulle hende i mel, for at finde den våde plet.*
  She's so fat that you have to turn her in flour to find the wet spot.

- *Hun er sgu' en sild.*
  She's a damn nice looking fish (chick).

- *Du ligner en ged og du lugter af tis.*
  You look like a goat and you smell of piss.

- *Du er så grim at du gør blinde børn bange.*
  You are so ugly you scare blind children.

- *Du ser ud som om der er en der har fået tændt ild i dit ansigt, og har slukket det med en kæde.*
  You look like someone has lit a fire on your face, and put it out with a chain.

- *Behøver du virkelig være så grim?*
  Do you have to be that ugly?

French

- *Sais-tu combien de temps ta mère prend pour chier? Neuf mois!*
  Do you know how much time your mother needs to take a shit? Nine months!

- *Faut péter dans l'eau pour faire des bulles.*
  Go to fart in water and make bubbles.

- *Le cerveau il etait en option chez toi.*
  The brain was optional for you.

- *T'as une tête a faire sauter les plaques d'egouts.*
  You've got a face that would blow off manhole covers.

- *Combien tu prends pour hanter une maison?*
  How much do you charge to haunt a house?

Hebrew

- *Im hayu samim et hamo'ach shelcha b'tarnegol, hu haya ratz yashar l'shochet.*
  If they had to put your brain in a chicken, it would run straight to the butcher.

- *Ya smark shel ez!*
  You piece of a goat's spittle!

- *At tachat shel dog mishuga gadol.*
  You are a crazy big fish's ass.

- *Lekh taaseh amidat yadaim al hagag, vetekhavan et hazain layareah.*
  Go stand on your head on the roof and point your dick at the moon.

- *Im hatipshut hayta etz, ata hayita chorshat kakal!*
  If stupidity was a tree, you would have been a forest!

Italian

- *Aricchi Du Porcu.*
  You are similar to hair on a pig's ear.

- *Cagati in mano e prenditi a schiaffi.*
  Shit in your hand then slap yourself in the face.

- *Se il cazzo avesse le ali, la tua fica sarebbe un aereoporto.*
  If dicks had wings, your pussy would be an airport.

Japanese

- *Kisama.*
  Lord of the donkeys.

- *Baba kusai.*
  Old woman smell.

- *Debou wa ase o taksan kakimasu.*
  Fat people sweat a lot.

- *Obatarien.*
  An overbearing, nagging woman.

- *Issunboshi.*
  One Inch Boy (refers to penis size).

- *Anata no ketsu wa kusa da oyobi ore wa shibakariki da.*
  Your ass is grass, and I'm the lawnmower.

Latin

- *Te futueo et caballum tuum. [ALSO: "Te futueo et equum tuum"]*
  Screw you and the horse you rode in on.

- *Es stultior asino.*
  You are dumber than an ass.

- *Tum podem extulit horridulum.*
  You are talking shit.

- *Stultus est sicut stultus facit.*
  Stupid is as stupid does.

Moroccan

- *Hamar li Waldik.*
  Your father is a donkey.

- *Allah inaal din Tabon Imok.*
  Allah curse the religion of your Mother's pussy.

- *Malik maloof.*
  Your king is a pig.

Somali

- *Hooyadaa waxay urtaa sida malayga.*
  Your mother smells like fish.

- *Sharmutaada ayaa ku dhashay was!*
  Fuck the whore that birthed you!

Spanish

- *Tu madre tiene un bigote.*
  Your mother has a moustache.

- *El dumbass más grande en el mundo.*
  The biggest dumbass in the world.

- *Cuando monos vuelven de mi culo.*
  When monkeys fly out of my ass.

- *Mermelada de huevas.*
  Extremely idiotic person. (lit. testicle jelly)

- *Siembrate una mata!*
  Plant a tree on your head! (a bald person)

Trinidadian

- *Pika in she nany she cya geh a man.*
  Her pussy is so bad she can't get a man.

- *Pantyman.*
  Faggot.

Turkish

- *Ananin amina cam dikerim, golgesinde seni sikerim trans.*
  I will plant a pine tree into your mom's pussy and fuck you in its shade.

- *Ananin aminda sampanya patlattik.*
  We opened a bottle of champagne in your mother's pussy.

Welsh

- *Cadwch Cymru yn lan. Danfonwch y sbwriel i Loegr!*
  Keep Wales Tidy. Leave Your Rubbish in England!

- *Bronnau fel bryniau Eryri.*
  Tits like the mountains of Snowdon.

- *Rwyt ti'n esgys fach pathetic am dyn.*
  You're a pathetic little excuse for a man.

- *Twpsyn.*
  Idiot.

- *Pisho bant.*
  Piss off.

Yiddish

- *Eyn imglik iz far im veynik.*
  One misfortune is too few for him.

- *Shteyner zol zi hobn, nit kayn kinder.*
  She should have stones and not children.

- *Azoy fil ritzinoyl zol er oystrinkn.*
  He should drink too much castor oil.

- *Zalts im in di oygen, feffer im in di noz.*
  Throw salt in his eyes, pepper in his nose.

- *Shteyner af zayne beyner.*
  Stones on his bones.

- *Trinkn zoln im piavkes.*
  Leeches should drink him dry.

- *Lakhn zol er mit yashtherkes.*
  He should laugh with lizards.

- *A hiltsener tsung zol er bakumn.*
  He should grow a wooden tongue.

- *Krugn zol er di (town name here) brokh.*
  He should get the (town name here) hernia.
- *Fransn zol esn zayn layb.*
  Venereal disease should consume his body.

- *A meshugener zol men oyshraybn, un im araynshraybn.*
  They should free a madman, and lock him up.

- *Golem.*
  A clumsy and sluggish person.

- *Kucker.*
  Shit head.

RESOURCES

Much of the more general material is freely available in the public domain, and the author would like to thank the following sites for their inspiration.

www.aciddrops.com

www.anecdotage.com

www.braincandy.com

www.brainyquote.com

www.brawl-hall.com

www.chavspotting.co.uk

www.comedyzone.net

www.corsinet.com

www.csvirginia.edu

www.insults.net (part of www.humourhub.com)

www.jokefile.co.uk

www.koalanet.com

www.multiplay.co.uk

www.one-linersandproverbs.com

www.peevish.co.uk

www.rateitall.com

www.quotationspage.com

www.thatsrich.com

www.the-top-tens.com

Where specific quotes have been used, every effort has been made to credit the appropriate source. If we have overlooked anybody, please feel free to get in touch and we will endeavour to rectify the situation.

Thanks are due to:

'Acid Drops' by Kenneth Williams – published by Orion

'Dictionary of Contemporary Quotations' by Jonathan Green – published by Pan Books

'Could Do Better' by Catherine Hurley – published by Pocket Books

Country Music titles compiled by Bill Atchley